KIDS CAN COPE

Say Hi When You're Shy

by Gill Hasson

illustrated by Sarah Jennings

free spirit
PUBLISHING®

Published in North America by Free Spirit Publishing Inc., Minneapolis, Minnesota, 2020

Library of Congress Cataloging-in-Publication Data
Names: Hasson, Gill, author. | Jennings, Sarah, illustrator.
Title: Say hi when you're shy / by Gill Hasson ; illustrated by Sarah Jennings.
Description: Minneapolis, MN : Free Spirit Publishing Inc., 2020. | Audience: Ages 6–9
Identifiers: LCCN 2020008210 | ISBN 9781631985690 (hardcover)
Subjects: LCSH: Bashfulness in children—Juvenile literature. | Social interaction in children—Juvenile literature.
Classification: LCC BF723.B3 H37 2020 | DDC 155.4/18232—dc23
LC record available at https://lccn.loc.gov/2020008210

Reading Level Grade 3; Interest Level Ages 6–9;
Fountas & Pinnell Guided Reading Level N

Edited by Alison Behnke and Marjorie Lisovskis

10 9 8 7 6 5 4 3 2 1
Printed in China
H13770420

Free Spirit Publishing Inc.
6325 Sandburg Road, Suite 100
Minneapolis, MN 55427-3674
(612) 338-2068
help4kids@freespirit.com
freespirit.com

First published in 2020 by Franklin Watts, a division of Hachette Children's Books · London, UK, and Sydney, Australia

Copyright © The Watts Publishing Group, 2020

The rights of Gill Hasson to be identified as the author and Sarah Jennings as the illustrator of this Work have been asserted in accordance with the Copyright, Designs and Patents Act, 1988.

Series editor: Jackie Hamley

Series designer: Cathryn Gilbert

Say Hi When You're Shy

by Gill Hasson
illustrated by Sarah Jennings

Turn the page to read about ways to feel more confident with other people.

Feeling shy?

What does it mean to be shy?

Do you ever get shy? It's not just you!
Everyone feels shy sometimes—even grown-ups.
We feel shy when we're not sure what to say or do around other people. We can feel nervous when we try something new, or until we get used to doing something.

What if I do it wrong and they all laugh at me?

Sometimes being shy can also mean we are good at paying attention and thinking things through.

3

How do you feel when you're shy?

When you're feeling shy, you might get worried or even scared. You might feel embarrassed and uncomfortable. You might worry about looking silly to other people.

Maybe your face gets hot and your heart starts thumping. Your legs go all shaky and your stomach feels fluttery.

4

Sometimes you might feel sad or lonely because you want to join in with other children but your shyness holds you back.

Other times, you might just want to be on your own but worry that this will upset other people or that they won't invite you to join in next time.

What happens when you feel shy?

When you're with other kids, you might be quiet and not say much to them. Maybe you watch others play, but you don't join in.

You might feel shy around grown-ups too.
Maybe you find it difficult to speak up,
so you mumble, whisper, or say nothing at all.

It can feel like your tongue is tied. You might look at the ground and think that you just want to shrink or be left alone.

Hello, Leo.
How is your new school?

Erm...

7

It's okay to feel shy!

If you often feel shy, it might take time for you to feel comfortable in new situations and with new people.

Maybe you like to watch for a while before you feel ready to join in.

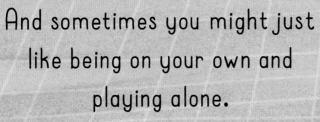

And sometimes you might just like being on your own and playing alone.

That's okay!

There could also be times when you do want to join in but you don't know how to get past your shyness.
You're not sure what to say or do.
And this might mean you feel left out.

Come and sit with us!

Don't hide because you're shy! There are things you can do. You can learn to be more confident and comfortable around other people.

Knowing what to say

Think about how you feel around people you're not shy with. These are probably people you know well, like your mom or dad, a brother or sister, or a good friend.

When you're around friends and family you feel comfortable with, you talk clearly in a voice they can hear.

Pass the ketchup, please!

You feel relaxed and safe telling them what you do and don't want. You ask them things and you answer their questions. You're friendly and you don't have to think about how to talk to them or what to say.

You can learn to do this more easily with other people too.

Taking steps to feel less shy

To start with, think of some things you feel too shy to do or say and write them down. Then choose one thing that you're just a bit uncomfortable about doing.

Try to come up with ideas for how to do this without feeling so shy. There are ideas in this book to help you. Practice doing that one thing until you feel better about it. Then move on to the next thing on your list.

12

Jenna wrote down things that she was shy about doing. There were some things she felt a bit shy about, and others she felt really shy about. Then Jenna started on the first thing she felt a bit worried about and came up with some ideas to help her feel happier and more comfortable doing it.

Invite a friend to your home

If you feel awkward around other children, you might find it easier to be with just one person rather than lots at the same time. So you could try starting with one friend.

Sometimes it can be easier to be with a new friend in your own home, where you feel most comfortable and relaxed. Perhaps you could invite another child to your home to play for a couple of hours. Before your friend arrives, think about some things you could do together that you might both enjoy.

Once your friend is there, try to make them feel welcome.

Ask what your friend would like to play. You could suggest some of the things to do together that you thought of earlier.

Plan ahead for parties

Sometimes you'll want to go to places where there will be lots of people. This can be fun—but it can be scary too.

Omar was worried about feeling shy at his friend Ana's party. There would be other kids there who he didn't know.

Omar and his mom decided to practice what he could do. They set up an imaginary party with Omar's toys and pretended that one of the toys was shy. Omar showed the toy what to do and say.

If you are worried about being shy at a party or another event, ask a grown-up or a friend to help you plan a few simple things you could say. This can help you feel more prepared and happier about going. Other people might also be feeling shy there, just like you. Maybe you'll even help someone else feel less shy!

Join something you like doing

Sometimes you might find it easier not to feel shy if you can join in with something you really like doing. You don't have to do that thing on your own.

You might also feel better about joining a club or going to a new activity if you go with someone you know. Ask a friend if they'd like to go with you.

Perhaps you like gymnastics, soccer, basketball, or swimming. Or dancing and singing. Does your school have some after-school clubs? Maybe there's an art or games club you could go to.

When you join in with activities like these, you already have something to do and talk about with other people.

You might need to go a few times before you feel less shy. That's fine. Keep trying, and don't give up.

When you feel shy around adults

Talking to grown-ups isn't always easy.
A good idea is to ask someone else to help you
think of some simple things you could say in
different situations.

Lizzie and her grandma practiced ways Lizzie
could talk to adults. Each time, she remembered
to look at the other person and speak clearly
in a voice the other person could hear.

Saying what you do and don't want

There are some situations where it can be really difficult to say what you do or don't want.

But that's my ball!

You might find it hard to say that you don't like something or don't want to do something.

It can also feel scary to say that you don't understand something and need some help.

You may worry that others won't listen to you or that they might make fun of what you say.

Practice speaking up

Even when it's hard, sometimes you need to speak up!

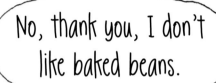

No, thank you, I don't like baked beans.

Speaking up means saying what you do or don't want in a polite but firm way.

I'm not sure how to do the homework. Can you please tell me what I need to do?

If there's something that is important to you but that
you find difficult to speak up about, you could ask
a grown-up or a friend to help you practice saying it.
It can help to practice in the mirror on your own too.

Build up
your courage

What you need and what you do or don't want matter.
If you don't want to do something or you need help,
you can say something!

You will need a bit of courage. That means doing something
even though you feel a little bit scared.

You can tell yourself, "I can do this," and "It will be okay."
Take a big breath and then as soon as you breathe out,
look at the other person. In a voice the other person can hear,
say what you do or don't want or what you need.

You might be surprised at how good it feels to speak up.
And each time you speak out, you will feel
more and more confident.

Say Hi When You're Shy

We feel shy when we're not sure what to say or do around other people. It might take a little while for you to warm up and feel comfortable in new situations and with new people. And sometimes you might just prefer to be on your own. That's fine! But when you do want to join in and talk to other people, you can learn to be more confident and comfortable. Here are some reminders:

- Ask a grown-up or a friend to help you plan a few simple things you could say in situations where you feel shy. Practice together until it feels easier for you.
- Try inviting a new friend to your home. Make them feel welcome and do some things together that you'll both enjoy.
- Think of an activity you really like doing, and find ways that you could join in with other children who are doing it. Ask a friend if they'd like to go with you.
- When you need to speak up, tell yourself, "I can do this." Take a big breath, look at the other person, and, in a voice the other person can hear, say what you do or don't want.

And remember, you can always start by saying hi!

Now you know it's okay to feel shy.

And you know how to help yourself feel more comfortable around others.

28

Activities

- Draw or write about something you feel shy about joining in with.

- Draw your shy face. Then draw your friendly face.

- Kira is worried about feeling shy when she goes to her friend's picnic.
  What do you think Kira could do to help her feel less worried about it?
  Write Kira a letter with some ideas about what she can do or say at the picnic.

- Anton is worried about standing up in class next week when it's his turn to do
  show-and-tell. Write him a letter with an idea for what he could do to feel
  more prepared and less shy.

- Think of a situation where you often feel shy. Draw a picture of yourself in
  that situation, looking confident and happy.

- Ask a grown-up what they were shy about when they were a kid. Ask them
  what happened that helped them feel less shy. Draw a picture or write a story
  about it.

- Write down some things you can say to yourself to help you have courage when
  you need to speak up about what you do or don't want.

Notes for teachers, parents, and other adults

It's natural to want the children you care for to feel at ease with others and to have confidence in social situations, so it's also natural to feel frustrated when some children feel shy, are slower to warm up, or get worried about joining in with other children or talking to adults. If you are concerned that a child is very shy, it's important that you avoid labeling that child as shy or nervous, either directly to them or when talking about them to others. Labels can stick and may become self-fulfilling prophecies. If you label a child as shy, you give them permission to stay in their shell, and their anxiety about social situations may grow. Instead, give them other ways to think about themselves. You could say, for example, "It's fine if it takes a little while for you to feel comfortable with new people." "You like to listen to others and watch what's happening first before you join in." "It's good that you talk easily with people you know well. People like Principal Navarro and . . ." Also try not to step in too much when a child is feeling shy. Resist, for example, the urge to respond to a question another adult asks the child; instead, encourage the child to look at the adult and answer the question themselves.

Children also benefit from knowing effective techniques to help them take control of their feelings and worries. *Say Hi When You're Shy* explains ways children can cope with feeling shy. You can help them learn and practice some of these strategies. For example, you could help a child rehearse ahead of time for a situation that makes them nervous, like going to a birthday party or meeting new people. You can also help them come up with ideas for activities they'd feel at ease with doing with other children.

Although children can read this book by themselves, it will be more helpful if you read it together. You could talk about situations that you find daunting and how you manage them. For example, "Sometimes I feel worried about speaking up at a meeting, but then I take a deep breath and say something and I feel good about sharing my thoughts." As you read the book, ask children questions such as: "Have you felt like that?" "What do you think of that idea?" "How could that work for you?" "How do you think the people in this picture are feeling?"

After reading the book and helping children identify some strategies that could work for them, give them the opportunity to manage situations at their own pace and with your support. With time, patience, and encouragement from you, children can learn to cope with feeling shy and learn to be more confident around others. However, if their shyness, worries, and fears are frequently causing them distress and leading them to avoid everyday situations and miss out, it's worth seeking more advice. Reach out to a healthcare provider, a counselor, or another expert and ask for help.